Cambridge Discovery Readers

Level 2

Series editor: *Nicholas Tims*

Killer Bees

Jane Rollason

CAMBRIDGE
UNIVERSITY PRESS

CAMBRIDGE
UNIVERSITY PRESS

University Printing House, Cambridge CB2 8BS, United Kingdom

One Liberty Plaza, 20th Floor, New York, NY 10006, USA

477 Williamstown Road, Port Melbourne, VIC 3207, Australia

314–321, 3rd Floor, Plot 3, Splendor Forum, Jasola District Centre, New Delhi – 110025, India

103 Penang Road, #05-06/07, Visioncrest Commercial, Singapore 238467

Cambridge University Press is part of the University of Cambridge.

It furthers the University's mission by disseminating knowledge in the pursuit of education, learning and research at the highest international levels of excellence.

www.cambridge.org

This American English edition is based on *Killer Bees*, ISBN 978-84-832-3503-4 first published by Cambridge University Press in 2009.

© Cambridge University Press 2009, 2010

First published 2009
American English edition 2010
Third printing 2011

20 19 18 17 16 15 14 13 12 11 10 9 8 7

Printed in Great Britain by CPI Group (UK) Ltd, Croydon CR0 4YY

ISBN 978-0-521-14896-2 Paperback American English edition

Illustrations by Albert Asensio

Audio recording by hyphen

Exercises by Jane Rollason

The publishers are grateful to the following for permission to reproduce photographic material:

Getty Images | David Scharf for cover image

Contents

People in the story

Jo Fisher: a fifteen-year-old schoolgirl
Martha Fisher: Jo's mom; she works and takes care of her
two daughters
Amy Fisher: Jo's younger sister; she goes to a different
school from Jo
Merlin: Jo's dog; he's a German Shepherd dog and is very
intelligent
Mikey: a friend of Jo's; he's a year older than Jo and goes to
the same school as her
Sean: a nineteen-year-old boy that Jo meets
Gus: a man from Boston in the northeast of the United
States
Sam: Amy's best friend; he lives in the house next door

BEFORE YOU READ
● ●

1 Look at the cover and the pictures in the first two
chapters. Answer the questions.
   1 Where do you think the story happens?

....

   2 Can you predict three things that happen in this part of the
   story?

....

Chapter 1

A car ride

"You can't go out tomorrow night, Jo!" shouted Jo's mom. "You have to take care of Amy for me."

"But I *want* to go out," Jo shouted back.

"Jo, I work all week. I want one night out," said her mom.

"*I* work all week. I want to go out with my friends."

Jo went into the kitchen. Breakfast was short and loud. BANG! She put her plate on the table. BANG! She shut the refrigerator door.

The radio was on. They were playing an old song by The Killers. Then it was the news. Jo went to get her bag from her room. She came back into the kitchen.

"*... escaped after scientists ...*" the radio was saying. She turned it off.

BANG! She put the coffee back in the cupboard.

"Stop it, Jo!" shouted her mom from the living room. "You'll break something!"

Jo called Merlin. The dog ran up to her and she put her arms around his neck.

"I love you, Merlin," she said.

BANG! went the front door.

Jo walked down the road to the bus stop and then stopped.

"Oh no!" she thought. She remembered her English homework. It was on her bed in her room. "Mr. Bates will kill me. I'll have to go back. Now I'll be late."

She walked back to the house. Her mom and sister were coming out.

"What's wrong?" said her mom.

"My homework's upstairs," said Jo.

"Oh, Jo! You never think!"

"Can you take me to school?" she asked her mom.

"We're going with Sam and his mom today. There isn't room for you in their car."

"Thanks a lot," said Jo angrily and she went into the house.

"And remember to take the dog for a walk when you get home," shouted her mom.

A few minutes later Jo came out of the house again. Mikey was going by.

"Hey, Jo," he called. "How are things?"

"Yeah, OK," said Jo. Mikey came up to the front door.

"You don't look very happy," he said.

"Oh, you know," said Jo. "My mom never lets me do anything."

"Do you have time for coffee?" he asked.

"We'll be late for school," Jo replied.

Jo liked Mikey. He was in the grade above her and he lived on the next street. He was always in trouble at school, but he was funny. And today, "funny" was good.

"What's your first class?" asked Mikey.

"What day is it? Thursday. It's math," said Jo.

"Math is boring," said Mikey.

She thought about math. "OK, then. I'll go into school after math."

They had coffee in the kitchen. Jo put the radio on again. They were talking about bees, so she turned it off.

"Who wants to know about bees?" said Mikey. He looked out of the window. Jo's mom's car was in front of the house.

"Hey, I have an idea!"

"Oh, yeah? What's your idea?" asked Jo.

"Can you drive?" asked Mikey. He didn't wait for an answer. "*I* can," he said. "I drive my dad's car all the time."

"I'm not old enough," said Jo. "But I *have* ridden a scooter [1]."

"Let's go out in your mom's car. Your mom won't know. We'll drive around for ten minutes and then come back. Come on!"

"Mikey, that is the worst idea …" Jo said.

"Come on, it'll be fun," Mikey said.

"Why shouldn't I have some fun?" she asked herself. People shouted at her all day – at home, in school.

"What will my mom say?" she said.

"She won't know," said Mikey.

"People will see us," Jo said.

"Nobody will see us – everyone's at work or in school," said Mikey. "Where are the car keys?"

She pulled on her big winter coat over her clothes. Mikey was already in the car. She got in beside him.

"I don't believe this," Jo said. "Why are we doing this?"

"You were feeling sad. Remember?" said Mikey. "Now you're having a fun day! Ready?"

"OK, let's do it," she said.

Mikey started the car. He drove carefully down the road and stopped at a red light. He turned left and started to drive out of town.

"What do you think?" he asked.

"What do I think about what?" Jo said. She was beginning to feel sick.

"Am I a good driver?" Mikey said. He was smiling.

"Mikey, this is really stupid," said Jo.

He started to drive faster. Jo was really afraid now.

"Mikey, can we turn around, please? Now! This isn't funny."

Mikey laughed.

They were in the country now. They drove through some woods.

"How fast can this car go?" said Mikey.

"Mikey, stop! Please stop the car."

"Watch this!" he said. The car went faster.

"Mikey! Stop!"

Then the road turned to the right. Mikey tried to turn but he was going too fast.

"MIKEY!" Jo screamed.

The car went off the road and into the woods. It went faster and faster between the trees. Jo and Mikey banged their heads on the roof. They were screaming. Then there was a tree right in front of them …

Jo opened her eyes. Everything was quiet. There was a smell of smoke. She opened her door and got out. She went around to Mikey's side and opened his door. His eyes were

closed. She put her hand on him. He moved. He wasn't dead.

"Come on, Mikey," she said. Mikey opened his eyes for a moment, but then closed them again.

"Wake up!" she shouted at him.

But he didn't. Jo looked for her phone.

"Oh no!" she thought. "I left it in the kitchen."

She found Mikey's phone in his pocket. She called 911 and asked for help.

"There's been an accident," she said. "It was a boy in a car. He's not dead, but his eyes are closed."

She told them where the car was.

"What's your name?" asked the woman.

But Jo couldn't say her name. She couldn't say, "I was in the car, too." This was starting to feel like a bad dream.

"My name's …" she started to say. "I had nothing to do with it … I was just walking my dog in the woods."

"OK. Can you wait there for an ambulance?"

"Yes, I'll wait."

Jo put Mikey's phone back in his pocket.

Fifteen minutes later Jo heard the ambulance. She sat high in a tree, about fifty meters from the car. She didn't move.

Two paramedics got out of the ambulance.

"Did he break anything?" asked one of the men.

"I don't think so," said the other.

They carried Mikey to the ambulance.

"Who called us?" one of them asked.

"A woman," said the other. They looked around quickly.

"Was she in the car, too?"

"No. She said she saw the accident. She was walking her dog. Do you want to look for her?"

"No, let's get back," said the first one, "the soldiers² are coming and they ..."

Jo couldn't hear the end of the sentence.

Chapter 2

The farm

Jo waited in the tree. But nobody came for the car. She climbed down the tree and jumped³ into soft leaves.

"Ow!" she said and put her hand to her neck. She looked at her mom's little red car. And then she was sick.

She suddenly felt angry with her mom.

"Why didn't she take me to school?" she thought. "She never does anything for me. Everything's for Amy. Now look what's happened."

Jo started to walk, but not to the road. She went into the woods. Weak sunlight fell through the trees around her. The air was cold, but Jo was warm in her big coat. Her mouth was dry. She had no water, no food, no phone, and not much money. She walked for some time.

After a while, she sat down to think.

"I can't go home," she said to herself. "Mom will be really angry now. I can't go to school. They'll find out about the car and Mikey. I'll have to leave. Maybe I can find a place to sleep tonight. Then tomorrow I can go to New York. I'll get a job and find a room in a house. I can start a new life."

She got up and walked on. Soon the trees came to an end. Jo looked across the open country. There was a farm⁴ about a kilometer away. It had lots of buildings.

"I can sleep there tonight," she thought. She walked toward the farm. It was about a quarter to six. The sun was already going down. As she got closer to the farm, there were some apple trees. Food! She ate an apple and put some more in her coat pockets. Then she sat down to wait for the dark.

A few minutes later lights went on in the farmhouse. Then a car arrived – two children jumped out and ran into the house. A woman followed them. A man and a black and white dog came out of the house and went into one of the big farm buildings. Jo heard the sound of cows.

Jo pulled her coat around her.

"I haven't worn this for a long time," she thought.

The coat had lots of pockets. She found her house key, bus tickets, and an old picture of her with her parents. It was just before her dad died. And in the inside pocket, she found a very old chocolate bar.

"I'll eat half now and keep half for later," she thought.

But she ate it all.

* * *

It was really dark now. The woman and children came out of the house with bags and boxes. The children got in the car. The man and the dog came back and the dog jumped into the car. The woman put her arms around the man. They talked for a long time before the woman got into the car. The man watched them drive away.

Jo was cold now and she walked down to the farm. She went through the apple trees. Then she went down the side of the large farm building. The cows were moving around inside. She opened the door to a smaller building. There were no animals here, only bags of animal food. She made herself a bed with empty bags at the back of the building. Moonlight came in through a dirty window.

It was a long night and she slept badly. Three times she heard something run over the bags of animal food. Was it a rat? She didn't like rats and she pulled her coat over her head.

It began to get light. She heard someone outside the door. Then the door opened. Jo didn't move. She couldn't see the door from her bed.

Someone opened a food bag.

"What's this?" said a man's voice.

He started to walk to the back of the building. What could he see? Jo pulled her coat up to her eyes.

And then his phone rang. Jo could hear her heart. It was beating loudly, but the man left the building. The door shut and she heard the key in the lock.

She waited for a few minutes and then looked out. The man was back by the house, but he was wearing a strange suit[5] – a beekeeper's suit.

Jo was afraid. But she had to get out. The window was old and easy to open. Jo climbed out into the daylight. She looked around the corner of the building. The man in the suit was going into the cow building. The cows were making a lot of noise.

"He'll be busy for some time," thought Jo.

There weren't any other people around. Jo ran to the farmhouse and went in through the back door.

For a moment, in the warm kitchen, Jo thought of her home and she wanted to cry. She took some bread and cheese from the table and put it in her pockets. She drank some milk.

Then she looked through the window and her heart almost stopped. The man was there. He was looking at her.

Jo turned and ran through the door and through the apple trees toward the woods.

Behind her the man shouted something. But Jo didn't stop. She ran like the wind.

LOOKING BACK

1 Check your answers to *Before you read* on page 4.

ACTIVITIES

2 Are the sentences true (*T*) or false (*F*)?

1 Jo wants to stay at home tomorrow night. $\boxed{F}$
2 Jo decides to go into school after the first class. ☐
3 Mikey isn't interested in bees. ☐
4 At first Mikey drives too fast. ☐
5 Jo's cell phone is in Mikey's pocket. ☐
6 Jo waits high in a tree for the ambulance. ☐
7 There are some apple trees near the farm. ☐
8 Jo finds some food in her pocket. ☐
9 Jo sleeps in the car that night. ☐

3 Match the two parts of the sentences.

1 Jo thinks about going $\boxed{e}$
2 Jo waits for the dark ☐
3 The woman, children, and dog drive away ☐
4 Jo hears rats ☐
5 Jo finds some breakfast ☐
6 The man sees Jo and she runs ☐

a in the farm kitchen.
b to the woods.
c during the night.
d to go to the farm.
e to New York.
f without the man.

18

4 Underline the correct words in each sentence.

1 Jo *likes* / *doesn't like* Mikey.

2 Jo is *older* / *younger* than Mikey.

3 Mikey *dies* / *doesn't die* in the accident.

4 Jo calls *her mom* / *an ambulance* after the accident.

5 The paramedics *don't know* / *know* who called them.

6 Jo *sleeps* / *doesn't sleep* well that night.

7 The next morning Jo *doesn't want* / *wants* to go home.

8 The *woman* / *man* finds Jo in the farmhouse.

5 Answer the questions.

1 Why does Jo have to go back to the house in Chapter 1?

To get her English homework.

2 Whose car does Mikey drive?

3 What does Jo find in her pockets?

4 How does Jo get out of the farm building?

LOOKING FORWARD

6 What do you think? Answer the questions.

1 In Chapter 3, Jo finds someone she knows. Who is it?

2 In Chapter 4, Jo goes on a long journey. Why?

Chapter 3

Going home

Jo looked back. The farmer wasn't following her.

"Maybe he'll call the police," she thought. So she didn't stop. She walked all day along a small river. There were a few houses on the way, but nobody was home. There were some chickens behind one house. They were hungry. When Jo gave them some food, she saw three eggs. The garage was open and Jo found some matches. She cooked the eggs over a fire on an old tin plate. They tasted good!

When she was too tired to walk, she found a soft place under some trees. She made a sort of bed and was soon asleep. Strange animals woke her in the night. They made more noise than cars and buses.

She woke again at first light. A small bird was looking at her.

"This is not real," she said to herself. But her empty stomach told her it was real. "I'll go home," she said to the bird. "Mom will shout at me, but right now, I don't care. I need food and a warm bed."

After another kilometer, a road crossed the river. She knew the road – it wasn't far from home.

She ran down the road.

"When a car comes, I'll stop it," she thought.

But no cars came.

"What day is it? Saturday? Where is everyone?" she thought.

Then she saw something strange far away. It was high in the air. It was like a cloud, but it was going around and around. Was it making a noise? She listened, but she couldn't really hear anything.

There were houses now and she came into the town. It was so quiet. There were no people.

"Have I traveled in time? What's happened to the world?" she thought.

She looked all around as she walked. Finally she got to her house. It looked normal.

Jo unlocked the front door and went in. There wasn't a sound. No one was home. She went to the kitchen and got some food out of the refrigerator. The light wasn't working and the refrigerator wasn't cold, but she didn't think about it. She ate the food quickly.

Then she went upstairs and looked at herself in the mirror. "Argh!" she screamed. "My hair!"

Jo showered. The water was almost cold. She put on some clean, warm clothes, and got into bed.

"Mom will be home soon," she thought. "I don't care if she's angry. I'm safe now." And she fell fast asleep.

Many hours later Jo woke up. Moonlight was coming in through the window. What time was it?

A car went by. She ran to the window and saw red lights turn the corner. She tried her bedside light, but it didn't work. She ran down to the kitchen. The lights didn't work. The clock on the wall said five o'clock.

"Is it five in the morning or five in the afternoon?" Jo thought.

She found a flashlight[6] in a cupboard. There was her phone on the kitchen table. She ran and turned it on. There were four messages, two from her mom. The first message was sent on Thursday at lunchtime.

```
Sorry I shouted. Hope you weren't late for
school! Love Mom xx
```

The second was sent on Thursday at 5:30.

```
Where are you? Where's the car? We have to
go. Everyone's going. Call me right now.
```

The other two messages were from her friends. They wanted to know where she was.

Jo started to text her friends. "What's going on? Where is everyone?" But something was wrong. "Message not sent," her phone said.

She tried the TV. It didn't work. She tried the house phone. It was dead. And then she heard a noise at the back door. Someone was trying to get in!

Jo stood beside the door with her back to the wall. She had a kitchen knife in her hand. Her hands were hot. Her heart was beating fast.

There was the noise again. Then she knew what it was.

"Oh!" shouted Jo. She threw the knife on the table and unlocked the door.

A big black and brown dog ran into the kitchen.

"Merlin!" she screamed. Merlin barked[7] and jumped up. Jo put her arms around him and they sat on the floor. And then she cried.

Jo gave Merlin some food. He ate it in seconds.

"You're hungry, aren't you?" she said. "What's happened, Merlin? The world has changed. Everyone's gone ... except you and me. Why have they gone? Where have they gone? Why did they leave me behind?"

Jo's head hurt. They walked around the house with the flashlight. Jo was looking for the radio, but she couldn't find it. There were some letters on a small table by the front door and ... a note.

She read it.

Jo, we've got to go. The soldiers are telling everyone to go. Amy and I are traveling north because of the bees. The scientists think the bees can't live in the cold. If you're reading this, come north now. Amy and I have taken Merlin. We love you. We'll meet you when we get there. Got to go.
xxx Mom xxx

Jo sat on the floor. She had so many questions and no answers. She remembered the radio news, the farmer in the suit, the strange cloud in the sky.

"Were those bees?" she thought. "Are bees dangerous? I got a bee sting[8] once. I was fine." And then she looked at Merlin. "So how did you get here?"

It was still dark outside. Jo got up. "OK, think!" she said to herself.

She went upstairs for warm clothes and a sleeping bag. She got water and food from the kitchen. She put on comfortable sneakers.

She put the things in her school bag. Then she remembered Merlin and put in a bag of dog food.

She looked for something to write a note on. It was Amy's birthday last week and her birthday cards were on a table. She took one and wrote a note on the back.

Mom and Amy, if you get back before me, don't worry.
I'm following you north. I'll come home when it's over.
Merlin is with me. We're fine.

She put the note by the front door and put her big coat on. She went back to the note.

"I love you," she wrote at the end.

She put Merlin on his leash and stood by the front door.

"Ready?" she said to him. Then she screamed and Merlin barked.

Someone was banging on the front door.

Chapter 4

The journey begins

Jo ran to the back door to escape. She opened it and screamed again. A soldier was standing in front of her. He wore a special suit over his uniform and he had a gun.

"OK, Miss," he said. "What are you doing here?"

"I live here," said Jo. "This is my house."

"Is it? Or are you just looking through other people's things?"

"No!" Jo shouted. She showed him inside her school bag. "Look – here's my address. See?"

"Why are you here? Everyone from this area went north on Thursday afternoon. That's three days ago. Where's your family?"

"I was … away. I just came back," said Jo. "I don't know what's happening."

"It's been everywhere – on the TV, on the Internet – where have you been?"

"In the woods."

He looked at her closely for a moment.

"OK, come with me," he said. "It's getting light and you don't have a suit. We have to hurry."

Jo and Merlin followed the soldier to the front of the house. A small, dark cloud was in the sky above the house.

"Are those bees?" Jo asked.

The soldier looked up.

"Quick," he said. "Run!"

An army truck was waiting in the street. They climbed

into the back. There were more soldiers inside, a woman in a red sweater and a teenage boy. The first soldier jumped in and closed the back of the truck. The truck moved away fast.

Everyone looked through the back window. The cloud of bees came closer. They flew around the truck and it got darker inside. The woman screamed. Jo could hear the strange sound of the bees.

"Drive faster," shouted the soldiers. The truck turned onto a big, empty road and went really fast. They soon left the bees behind. Jo watched the cloud fly away.

"They're going," called the first soldier to the driver. "Good work."

"What happens if they sting you?" asked Jo.

"Don't you know about the bees?" the boy asked. "If they sting you, you die."

"No. I've been away," Jo said quietly. "And now I'm in some kind of bad dream."

She looked at the soldier.

"Where are we going?" she asked.

"Philadelphia," said the soldier. "Then we'll find you another truck. It will take you north to Canada."

"Is that your dog?" asked the boy.

"Yeah," said Jo. "My mom took him with her. But he came back for me."

Jo looked away and out of the back window.

"He's nice," said the boy. He put his hands in Merlin's thick hair.

"What's this around his neck?" he asked.

Jo looked. It was a note.

She quickly pulled it open and read it.

Jo, it's Thursday night. We're waiting in Philadelphia. I'm sending Merlin back for you. I didn't want to leave without you. They said I had to go. They're taking everyone to lots of different camps⁹ in Canada. Amy and I are going to Quebec City. Come and find us there. Get inside if you see any bees. Take food and water with you. Love, Mom and Amy

Jo wanted to cry but not in front of the boy. She looked out of the window again. There were small, dark clouds in the sky. The bees!

"What's wrong with these bees?" she asked.

"It's a long story," said the soldier. "In the last five years, millions of bees have died. It's a big problem. We need bees to grow[10] our fruit and vegetables. So, a few years ago, scientists started to study bees and change their genes[11]. They wanted to make them stronger. And then back in the spring some of the new bees escaped from a place in New York City."

"I didn't hear any news about the escape," said Jo.

"The government[12] didn't tell anyone," said the woman. "They couldn't find the bees. They thought the bees were dead."

"They *hoped* the bees were dead," said the soldier. "But these are smart bees. They moved into beehives[13] all over the country."

"And now they're everywhere – killer bees!" said the boy."

"They're mutants[14]," said the woman.

"This is like a science-fiction movie," said Jo. "And why aren't the phones working? And the TV?"

"We don't know," said the soldier. "We think it's the bees. Some radio stations work and people are using them to get information."

There was one question that Jo was afraid to ask. But she did.

"Have the bees killed anyone yet?" she asked.

"They started on Wednesday," said the soldier. "It was only a few people and some farm animals. But then more on Thursday. Then the government decided to move everyone to Canada. The scientists don't think that the bees can live in the cold and it's much colder in Canada. Right now, the bees are turning back before they get to Canada."

"Where's Quebec City?" she asked.

"It's in the east of Canada. We're going there, too," said the woman.

"Look!" the driver suddenly shouted. "There are millions of them! They're coming toward us!"

They all looked out of the window of the truck. The sky was almost black with a cloud of bees. The woman screamed. Jo put her arms around Merlin. The bees hit the left side of the truck. Some died as they hit the window. Jo could see them – they were long and black and yellow with long

stingers. They weren't like ordinary bees. The truck moved, but the driver stayed on the road. He drove faster. Everyone watched the cloud as it became smaller and smaller.

Jo was the first to speak. "Were they trying to push us over?" she asked.

"They've done that before," said the boy. "It was on the radio."

"Can they think?" Jo asked.

"We don't know," said the soldier.

"How are we going to stop them?" asked Jo.

For a moment no one said anything. Jo pulled Merlin closer to her.

"We don't know," said the soldier again.

LOOKING BACK

1 Check your answers to *Looking forward* on page 19.

ACTIVITIES

2 <u>Underline</u> the correct words in each sentence.

1 Jo sleeps the second night away from home *at the farm /* <u>*in the woods*</u>.

2 She *sees a few / doesn't see any* people on her way back to her house.

3 When she gets home, she goes to the *refrigerator / bathroom* first.

4 The first time Jo opens the back door, she sees *her dog / a soldier*.

5 Jo gets on a truck to *go back to the farm / escape from the bees*.

6 Jo has to meet her mom in *Quebec City / Philadelphia*.

7 The killer bees escaped from a place in *the United States / Canada*.

8 The bees *have already killed some people / haven't killed anyone yet*.

9 The bees *can / can't* live in cold weather.

3 Check (✓) the things that Jo takes on her journey.

1 a radio ☐
2 warm clothes ✓
3 a sleeping bag ☐
4 water ☐
5 a kitchen knife ☐
6 food for her ☐
7 food for Merlin ☐
8 a book ☐

4 Are the sentences true (*T*) or false (*F*)?

1 Jo isn't hungry when she gets home. ☐ *F*

2 There are no messages on Jo's phone. ☐

3 The truck can move faster than the bees. ☐

4 The truck is taking everyone to Canada. ☐

5 In the truck, the soldier asks Jo to complete a form. Complete it for her.

HOMELAND SECURITY FORM 6B: CHILD (under 18) WITHOUT PARENTS

Name: .... Last name: .... Age: ....

Parents: ....

Brothers and sisters: ....

Where are you traveling to?

....

Who are you traveling with?

....

---

6 Answer the questions.

1 Why does Jo decide to go back home?

....

2 Why is Merlin with Jo?

....

3 Why is everyone going to Canada?

....

LOOKING FORWARD

7 Check (✓) what you think happens in the next two chapters.

1 They get to Philadelphia safely. ☐

2 The bees kill some more people ☐

33

Chapter 5

Going north

The streets of Philadelphia were empty. There were more clouds of bees in the sky here. The truck took them to a small airport outside the town. As they waited outside a very large building, it began to rain. Some big doors opened and the truck drove in quickly. The doors shut behind them with a bang.

"Wow!" said the boy. "Look at all this!"

There was a line of big army trucks. There were mountains of boxes everywhere – medications[15], warm clothes, food, bottles of water, special suits.

"It's like on the TV," said Jo. "In other countries, I mean, after something terrible has happened."

"And now it's happening here," said the boy.

The soldier took Jo, the boy, and the woman over to another group of people.

"You're going to Boston with these people," said the soldier, "and then on to Canada."

"Can we eat something first?" asked the boy. "I'm really hungry."

"Sure," said the soldier. "You can't leave before it gets dark. The bees don't fly at night. I'm going to find some suits for you. The kitchens and bathrooms are over here." They followed him. The suits were too big, but they took them.

"There aren't many suits left," said the soldier. "Take care of them."

"Do they work?" asked Jo.

34

"Yes," said the soldier. "You're safe in the suits. The bees can't sting you through them."

*   *   *

Some hours later they got into the truck for Boston. Merlin jumped in with Jo.

"You're not bringing that dog," said one man to Jo.

"What?" said Jo.

"People come first now," said the man. "Animals have to take care of themselves."

"I'm not going anywhere without him," said Jo angrily.

"There's room for everyone and the dog," said one of the soldiers.

Jo sat beside the boy, with Merlin under the seat. The truck drove out into the night.

Everyone was afraid. Six soldiers sat behind the driver. They started to make jokes about the bees. It soon became hot in the truck and the woman with the red sweater fell asleep.

"I don't know your name," said Jo to the boy. "I'm Jo."

"Sean," he said. He was tall with black hair and gray eyes.

"What's going to happen to us, do you think?" Jo asked quietly. "Will we ever be able to go home again?"

"If they can find a way to stop the bees," said Sean.

"Will life ever be normal again?"

"Yeah, I'm sure it will," said Sean.

"You're lucky you have your mom with you," said Jo.

"You mean her?" said Sean and he pointed to the woman with the red sweater. "She's not my mom! Do I look like her? I don't think so!" Sean and Jo laughed quietly.

"She was already in the army truck when they found me," he said.

"So where's your family?"

"I live by myself."

"How old are you then?"

"Nineteen."

"Oh," said Jo. "I'm fifteen."

"I'm sure your mom didn't want to leave you," said Sean. "The soldiers told everyone to go. People couldn't say no."

"It's only four days since I saw them," said Jo. "It feels like four months."

"Where's your dad?" asked Sean.

"He died when I was ten," said Jo. "My sister was just a baby."

"What happened?"

"It was a car accident."

The truck slowed down and turned right.

"How terrible for your mom," said Sean.

"It was terrible for me, too," said Jo.

"Yes, but she had a new baby and lost her husband. That's hard. She was really happy and really sad at the same time."

In her head, Jo saw her mother beside her father's bed. They were in the hospital. Her mother had Amy in her arms and she was crying. She saw herself. She was ten years old and she sat in the corner. She didn't want to be there. She wanted to go home and play with her friends.

"Hey!" said Sean. He put his arm around her. "Don't cry."

"Am I crying?" asked Jo. "I didn't think I was crying."

"You'll find your family," said Sean. "Then you can start arguing with your mom again!"

They both laughed.

Suddenly the truck went more slowly. They heard strange noises on the road around them. People woke up.

"What's that noise?" asked one man.

"Don't worry," called the driver. "It's horses. They're running down the road."

Everyone looked out of the back of the truck. It was dark, but they could see the shapes of the horses. Some were gray, but they looked silver in the moonlight.

"Don't they look wonderful!" said Jo.

They traveled all night. The truck stopped for the drivers to change and to get food and water. It was still dark. They left the main road and drove into Boston.

"Look," said the woman with the red sweater. "There are people here."

A man was running down a side street. A door shut quickly. A car crossed in front of the truck.

"Lots of people have stayed here," said one of the soldiers. "They're living down in the Metro stations. That's why we're here. There have been a lot of problems."

"What kind of problems?" asked the woman.

"Stealing, fighting, shooting."

The truck drove through the city and stopped behind a big shopping mall. They waited outside a big building. The doors opened and they drove in. It was just like the one in Philadelphia.

They spent the day in the big building. They ate, slept, and listened to the news on the radio. The bees were still all over the United States, but not in Canada. The weather was warmer than usual. People were fine in the camps in Canada. Everyone was working well together. There were some problems with stealing and fighting in the big cities, like New York, Buffalo, and Boston.

One of the soldiers came to talk to them.

"Two of our people are going to take you on to Montreal," he said. "From there, you will go to different camps up in the north."

The big doors opened and they drove out into the dark.

"I'd like to see the sun again soon," said Jo.

They drove back across the city. Suddenly the driver stopped. Everyone in the back fell toward the front.

"What's happening?" someone screamed.

"Just keep quiet," said the driver.

Then the truck started moving from side to side. Merlin barked.

"Is it the bees again?" asked Jo.

"No," said Sean. "Look. It's people. They have guns."

Chapter 6

Escape

"Everyone out!" shouted a man in a long, black coat. He pointed his gun at the two soldiers. "Give us your guns. Get back to your army camp," he said to them. They didn't move. "Now!" he shouted. Two other men pointed their guns at the soldiers. The soldiers walked away with their hands in the air.

The man in the black coat spoke to everyone from the truck.

"We're not going to hurt you," he said. "We're just normal people. My name's Gus. We want to stay in Boston, that's all. The soldiers want us to leave. We live down in the Metro stations. We come out onto the streets at night. We get food and medication from the supermarkets."

"Why have you stopped us?" asked Sean.

"We want your truck, I'm afraid," said Gus. "We need it to move around in the daytime. Normal cars are no good here. The bees can push them over. We need those suits, too."

"Hey!" said Jo. "Those are ours."

Gus looked at Jo.

"Like I said, *we* need them," he said.

"What about us?" asked an older man from the truck. "We're going to Canada."

"Come with us," said Gus. "It's safer staying here."

There was no choice. Everyone from the truck agreed to follow Gus.

It was like a small town in the Metro station. Families and friends lived in their own areas. People smiled and said hello. There was an eating area and a TV was showing a children's movie.

"How do the lights work?" asked Jo.

"We have some smart people here," said Gus. "They can do anything."

"I like it here," said the woman with the red sweater. "It feels safe. Is there room for us?"

"Sure," said Gus. "You gave us a truck. We'll give you somewhere to live until it's all over."

"Can I go out at night?" asked Sean.

"Sure," said Gus. "You can go with the supermarket group."

"Can we leave if we want to?" asked Jo.

"We don't really want the soldiers to know about life down here. Once you're down here, we like you to stay." Gus smiled. But it wasn't a friendly smile.

Everyone agreed to stay.

Jo didn't say anything. She put her arms around Merlin.

"They'll never let us leave," she said in his ear. "We'll have to make a plan."

There was a locker near the Metro stairs. Gus put the bee suits in the locker. Jo was watching. An old man sat outside.

Later, Jo spoke to Gus. "Where's this supermarket, then?" she asked.

"We're going there now," he said. "Do you want to come?"

"Yeah," she said. And then she asked, "Can I have my suit?"

"You won't need it," Gus said. "We'll be back before it gets light. Let's go."

Jo and Merlin followed Gus and some other people from the Metro along dark streets. Jo tried to remember the street names. Then they came into a parking lot of a big supermarket. They walked over to a small door. Gus had a key.

"Yucky!" said Jo when they got inside. "What a smell!"

"The refrigerators aren't working," said Gus. "All the food is going bad."

Soon they were putting food and water into bags.

"Can I look around?" asked Jo.

"Sure," said Gus. "But we only take the things we need."

Jo and Merlin went to the sports department.

"Wow!" she said. "Look at those bikes."

She saw maps[16]. She looked for radios, but there weren't any.

On the other side of the supermarket, she found another door. It was like the one they came through. The key was in the lock. She took the key and put it in her pocket.

"OK, everyone," called Gus. "Back to the door."

When they got back to the Metro station, people came to look in the bags.

"Pasta again!" said a small boy. "Yucky!"

"Hey," said his mother, "this is wartime. You're lucky to have dinner."

Jo, Sean, and the other people from the truck found a place to put their things. They ate dinner. It was about 7:30 in the morning. Jo was beginning to feel tired. After only a few days in the station, everyone learned to sleep in the day and stay awake at night.

* * *

The next evening Jo got ready to leave. Gus, Sean, and the others went off to the supermarket. She went to talk to the man outside the locker with the suits. She sat beside him.

"You're doing a good job here," she said.

"It's boring," he said. "But someone has to do it. Were you watching that movie on the TV? I was, it was good."

"No, but we'll sit here for you," said Jo. "Merlin will

watch the locker. You go and watch the movie for half an hour."

"Are you sure?" he said. "That's really nice of you."

Twenty minutes later he came back.

"I enjoyed that," he said. "The end was great."

"Good," said Jo and she got up. "I'll see you at dinner."

"OK. Oh, and don't tell Gus about this, will you? He won't like it."

"I won't say a word," said Jo.

She went around the corner and found her bag. There was a second bag. It had her suit in. Then she ran up the stairs to the outside world. Merlin was right behind her.

"Where are you going?" asked a woman behind her.

"I'm just taking the dog out," said Jo. "He needs … you know. Gus told me to take him outside."

"OK," said the woman. "Don't be long."

They soon found the supermarket parking lot and waited behind some cars. Gus and the others came out of the side door. They walked across the parking lot, back toward the Metro station.

Ten minutes later Jo and Merlin were inside the supermarket. Jo chose the best bike and found a child's trailer.

"You can go in there when you're tired, Merlin," she said quietly. Then she quickly put food, water, and a map in the trailer.

An hour later Jo saw open country ahead. The only sound she could hear was the bicycle.

Bicycling was hard work. She often had to get off and walk.

"This is going to take weeks," she said to Merlin. But they didn't stop.

Jo looked at her watch. It was five in the morning. They needed somewhere to stay during the daytime. In the next town they saw a small hotel. Jo found a back door unlocked and they went in. There was a door under the stairs and there were more stairs behind it.

"Let's go down here," said Jo. "We'll be safe here." She pushed a box against the door from the inside. The room was black and cold. She turned on her flashlight. She took a look around and made a bed.

"Let's sleep now, Merlin."

She turned off the flashlight.

"I love you, Mom. I love you, Amy," she said into the dark. "We're coming."

LOOKING BACK

1 Check your answer to *Looking forward* on page 33.

ACTIVITIES

2 Put the sentences in order.

1 A soldier finds bee suits for Jo, the boy, and the woman. ☐
2 Jo tells Sean about her family. ☐
3 Jo and Merlin escape from the Metro station. ☐
4 Sean sees people with guns outside the truck. ☐
5 The army truck arrives in Philadelphia. ☐
6 They begin the journey to Boston. ☐
7 Jo goes to the supermarket with Gus. ☐
8 They are driving out of Boston when suddenly the truck stops. ☐
9 Everyone follows Gus into the Metro station. ☐

3 Are the sentences true (*T*) or false (*F*)?

1 There's no one in the streets when the truck gets to Philadelphia. ☐T☐
2 The bees don't sting people at night. ☐
3 The bees can't sting people through the bee suits. ☐
4 The woman with the red sweater is Sean's mom. ☐
5 Jo was a baby when her dad died. ☐
6 The man in the black coat has a gun. ☐
7 People can take anything from the supermarket. ☐
8 Jo takes her bee suit to Quebec City. ☐
9 The next night, Jo and Merlin don't sleep in the Metro station. ☐

4 Match the questions with the answers.

1 How did Jo's dad die? [d]

2 Why is Canada safer than the United States? ☐

3 Why does the woman in the red sweater want to stay in the Metro station? ☐

4 What does Gus do with the bee suits? ☐

5 Where does Jo find the bike? ☐

6 Where do Jo and Merlin spend the next night? ☐

a In a room under a hotel.

b The weather is colder there.

c He puts them in a locker.

d In a car accident.

e She feels safe.

f In the supermarket.

5 Answer the questions.

1 Where does Jo meet Sean?

....

2 What problems have there been in the big cities?

....

3 Why does Gus need the truck?

....

4 Why is there a bad smell in the supermarket?

....

LOOKING FORWARD

● ●

6 Check (✓) what you think happens in the next two chapters.

1 Gus and the others try to find Jo and Merlin. ☐

2 Jo arrives in Quebec City. ☐

Chapter 7

Quebec City

Jo and Merlin traveled by night. Winter was coming, but it wasn't as cold as usual for the time of year. A warm wind was coming from the south. They spent the days in empty farm buildings. After ten days they could see Montreal, but they didn't go into the city. There were more cars on the road here. They went off the road when they heard one.

"We don't want to meet another man like Gus," Jo said to Merlin. She looked out for an army camp, but they didn't see one.

There were lots of hills in this part of the country. Bicycling was hard work and Jo was very tired. Merlin rode in the trailer when they went down a hill. He had to run beside her when they went up a hill.

"It's two hundred and sixty kilometers to Quebec City from here, Merlin," she said on the eleventh morning. "I can't do it."

The light was breaking into the black sky. She wasn't wearing her suit, but she knew there were no bees in Canada.

They saw a small town below them. Merlin jumped in the trailer and they rode down fast. They had a walk around the town. Jo looked in all the garages.

"Merlin!" she shouted. "Look! That's what we want!"

There, inside a garage, was a scooter.

"I can ride a scooter!" she said.

The door wasn't locked and they went in.

"This will get us to Quebec City," she said to Merlin. "But where's the key?"

Jo found an unlocked window at the back of the house. She climbed in and found a box of keys in the kitchen. Five minutes later the scooter jumped into life.

Jo wrote a note.

I'm very sorry, but I'm taking your scooter. I have to find my family in Quebec City. When all this is over, I will save the money for the scooter and send it to you.
Thank you.
Jo

And she wrote her address.

Jo opened the garage door and she looked up at the blue sky. There was a big cloud of bees in front of them.

"Oh no!" she said. "But we're north of Montreal!"
She quickly shut the door and looked around the garage.
"Can the bees get in anywhere?" she said to Merlin.

She pulled a heavy box in front of the side door. She could see daylight under the main garage door. There were some old coats on the wall, so she pushed them under the door to stop the bees.

The bike was outside. Their food and water were in the trailer. Her suit was in the trailer.

"No dinner today, Merlin," she said. "But it'll be dark again soon. Let's sleep."

Jo's eyes were closing when it started. There was a loud noise. And then another and another. Merlin barked and ran from one side of the garage to the other. Jo ran to a little window in the side door. There were lots of small clouds of bees. They were all around the garage. They were flying into the door and the walls – fast.

Jo screamed as hundreds of bees hit the window. They were only centimeters away from her face.

The garage and the window were strong. After half an hour the bees stopped. Jo went back to the window and saw some dead bees. Their big black eyes and long stingers were horrible. They weren't like normal honey bees.

"I think they're gone," she said to Merlin.

They slept for some time. It was already dark when Jo woke up. She brought the trailer into the garage. It was much colder outside. Merlin started to bark at something in the corner.

"What is it?" Jo said. And then she heard the sound of a bee. It flew out of the corner and around the garage. Jo ran to get her suit. "Why didn't I put it on before?" she shouted.

The bee got louder and louder. And then it was quiet. Jo stopped moving and listened. Merlin barked.

"Shh!" she said. Something moved on her hand. And then it stung her.

"Ow!" she screamed. "No!"

She looked at her hand. There was a red mark and the skin was turning pink around it.

"Where's the bee?" she shouted. She looked around the garage.

"Ow, Merlin," she said. "My hand hurts."

But then she saw the bee. It was on the floor. It wasn't moving. It was dead. Jo looked at it. She was so happy that she started to cry. "Look, Merlin! It's a honey bee. It's a nice, friendly honey bee. It's not a killer bee!"

She put her arms around Merlin. She put her face in his soft, thick coat.

"OK, I'm ready," she said. She studied the map carefully. "We can do this trip by scooter in one night," she said to herself.

She put on a thick sweater and her big coat. She tied the

trailer to the scooter and they went outside.

"That wind's cold," said Jo. "It's coming from the north. Come on, Merlin. Let's go!" Merlin jumped into the trailer and Jo started the scooter.

She screamed with happiness as she rode the scooter quickly out of the town.

"This is the way to travel!" she shouted. The moon lit up the road.

They traveled all night. As they came near to Quebec City, Jo thought of her mom and Amy. "Will we find them? Will they be OK?"

The road climbed up ahead of them. Light broke through the clouds. When the scooter came to the top, Jo stopped and looked down. Her heart jumped. There, below them, was a city. But there were no buildings in this city. It was a city of tents and there were thousands of them. Then she heard shouting. There were people outside the tents. They were all looking up at the sky. Jo looked up, too. It was starting to snow.

Chapter 8

The camp

The snow was falling. Jo left the scooter behind some trees. She put Merlin on his leash and they walked down through the snow to the camp.

"I'm following *you* now, Merlin. Where's Mom? Where's Amy?" she said to him.

He started to pull and Jo followed him around the camp. People were dancing and laughing in the snow. Jo stopped to ask people, "Do you know Martha and Amy Fisher?" But nobody knew them.

"Try the information tent," someone said.

Jo found the tent. There were hundreds of pictures and messages. She looked at them all but didn't see her name. Jo felt like crying.

There was a woman in the tent, behind a desk.

"Name?" said the woman without looking up.

"I'm looking for my mother," Jo said.

She was crying now.

The woman looked up and smiled at Jo.

"I'm sorry. What's your name?" she asked and she put a hand on Jo's shoulder.

"Jo … Jo Fisher," she said.

The woman started looking through a long list of names. It was a few minutes before she looked up again.

"Yes, Martha Fisher. Your mother's here," she said finally. "And Amy Fisher."

Jo kissed the woman – she couldn't stop herself.

"But I don't know where they are," the woman said. "The camp gets bigger every day. Lots of people came yesterday from a camp near Montreal. The bees were coming closer yesterday."

"But they can't live in this cold, can they?"

"No. Don't worry. We heard on the radio this morning that the wind has changed and this cold weather is coming from the Arctic. It's moving south really fast. Most of the United States will soon be under snow. They think it's going to stay for weeks."

Jo couldn't wait any longer. She ran out of the tent.

"Thank you!" she called to the woman.

Jo and Merlin walked through the tents for another hour. And then Merlin started to pull. He stopped outside a tent and barked.

A face came to the door.

"Sam!" It was Sam from the house next door – Amy's friend.

"Where's Amy, Sam?"

"They're down there – not the next tent, not the next one, but the one after that," he pointed. "How did you get here? And Merlin!"

Sam put his little arms around Merlin.

Jo and Merlin walked by the next two tents. Merlin barked. She heard her mom's voice.

"Amy! That's Merlin! Merlin!"

"Merlin!" shouted Amy and the tent door opened. Amy's face looked out.

"Jo's here!" she screamed.

"What!" her mom shouted.

There was a lot of laughing and crying. Everyone from their street ran up and put their arms around Jo. Merlin barked at everyone.

Later, the four of them sat in the tent. Merlin rested his head on Amy. They drank tea and told their stories. Jo didn't tell her mom everything. She didn't want to worry her.

"I'm sorry, Mom," Jo said. "I'm sorry I ran away and crashed the car."

"Jo …," her mom started.

"No, Mom, listen. It's been difficult for you. I can see that now. And when Dad died and Amy was a baby, I never thought about you and how you felt. And, well, I'm sorry."

"You've had a long journey," said her mom.

"Yes, I've come a long way," said Jo.

Eighteen months later

"I don't have any clean clothes," shouted Jo from her bedroom.

"There are some in the closet by the bathroom," her mom shouted back from downstairs. "Your jeans are there, and some T-shirts. Try helping with the laundry[17] some time. Then you'll know where your clothes are."

Jo ran downstairs to the kitchen. She gave her mom a kiss.

"I help with the laundry sometimes. I put Amy's clothes away last week."

"Sure," laughed her mom. "Are you going out?"

"Yeah, Mikey's coming over and we're going ice-skating."

"Do you want me to drive you?" asked her mom.

"No, it's OK. We'll catch the bus."

She ran back upstairs. She opened the closet door. But then she stopped. There was a noise. She looked into the warm, dark closet. Something was moving. It was a … bee.

"Mom!" she screamed.

LOOKING BACK

●●

1 Check your answer to *Looking forward* on page 49.

ACTIVITIES

●●

2 Put the sentences in order.
1 Jo and Merlin find her mom and sister. ☐
2 Merlin finds Amy's friend, Sam. ☐
3 Jo and Merlin arrive in a town two hundred and sixty kilometers from Quebec City. ☐1☐
4 Jo finds a scooter in a garage. ☐
5 The bees try to get into the garage. ☐
6 Jo and Merlin travel all night to Quebec City. ☐
7 A honey bee stings Jo. ☐
8 Jo and Merlin arrive at the camp. ☐

3 Are the sentences true (*T*) or false (*F*)?
1 Jo is happy because she found a scooter to go to Quebec City. ☐T☐
2 Jo can't find the key to the scooter. ☐
3 Jo is badly hurt by the bee sting. ☐
4 When Jo and Merlin get to Quebec City, it starts to snow. ☐
5 Everybody in the camp knows Jo's mom. ☐
6 Jo can't find a message for her in the information tent. ☐
7 More people come to the camp every day. ☐
8 The snow is going to fall across most of the United States. ☐
9 The snow is only going to stay for a few days. ☐
10 Jo says sorry to her mom. ☐

4 Match the days of the story with the events.

1 Thursday (day 1) ☐6

2 Friday (day 2) ☐

3 Saturday (day 3) ☐

4 Sunday (day 4) ☐

5 Monday (day 5) ☐

6 Tuesday (day 6) ☐

7 Wednesday–Friday (days 7–16) ☐

8 Saturday (day 17) ☐

a Jo and Merlin travel to Quebec City.

~~b~~ Jo and Mikey crash Jo's mom's car. Jo spends the night at the farm.

c Jo finds her mom and sister.

d Jo goes home.

e Jo goes to Philadelphia in the army truck. That evening they leave for Boston.

f Jo walks all day and spends the night in the woods.

g In the evening, Jo escapes from the Metro.

h Jo and the others have to stop their journey to Canada.

5 Answer the questions.

1 Why is the snow a good thing?

....

2 Where is the cold weather coming from?

....

3 Who does Merlin find first?

....

4 Why doesn't Jo tell her mom everything?

....

5 Eighteen months later, what does Jo see in the closet?

....

Glossary

[1]**scooter** (page 8) *noun*   a small motorcycle

[2]**soldier** (page 12) *noun*   a person who fights for their country

[3]**jump** (page 13) *verb*   to push your body into the air using your feet

[4]**farm** (page 13) *noun*   a place where a farmer keeps animals and grows vegetables and fruit

[5]**suit** (page 17) *noun*   (here) special clothes to keep bees out

[6]**flashlight** (page 23) *noun*   a small light that you can carry in your hand

[7]**bark** (page 23) *verb*   when a dog barks, it makes loud noises

[8]**bee sting** (page 25) *noun*   if you have a bee sting, a bee has put its poison in your skin

[9]**camp** (page 28) *noun*   a place where people stay in tents

[10]**grow** (page 29) *verb*   to put a plant in the ground and take care of it

[11]**gene** (page 29) *noun*   every living thing has genes; your genes decide what you are like; you get your **genes** from your parents

[12]**government** (page 29) *noun*   the group of people who control a country

[13]**beehive** (page 30) *noun*   a place where bees live

[14]**mutant** (page 30) *noun*   a mutant bee, for example, is different from other bees because its genes have changed

[15]**medication** (page 34) *noun*   the doctor gives you this when you are sick

[16]**map** (page 45) *noun*   a picture that shows where countries, towns, and roads are

[17]**laundry** (page 60) *noun*   clothes and sheets that have to be washed